AVERY PEAK

A Life Less Black and White

Copyright © 2025 by Avery Peak

All rights reserved. No part of this publication may be reproduced, stored or transmitted in any form or by any means, electronic, mechanical, photocopying, recording, scanning, or otherwise without written permission from the publisher. It is illegal to copy this book, post it to a website, or distribute it by any other means without permission.

First edition

This book was professionally typeset on Reedsy.
Find out more at reedsy.com

Contents

Acknowledgments — vi

1. Be Enough. You Aren't Too Much. — 1
2. The Stars Were My Friends. — 2
3. Lack of Love, Mostly Malice. — 4
4. Mockingbird. Fragile Bird. — 6
5. My Temple Has Stained Glass. — 8
6. Pretended To Want Me. — 9
7. Let The Games Begin. — 10
8. No Means No, Even If Soft — 14
9. Speak To Me. — 16
10. The Holes You Left Were Smaller. — 17
11. I Fight. — 19
12. Stand Strong. — 21
13. Sparrow's Song. — 23
14. Hummingbird Wings. — 24
15. Lacking. — 25
16. No One. Nothing. — 28
17. Phoenix Rising. — 29
18. Palpable Air. — 30
19. Betrayed By Memory. — 31
20. Screaming Silence. — 33
21. Give More. — 34
22. Shameless Remorse. — 36
23. Fuck The Ocean. — 38

24	You Sparked Life Back Into Me.	39
25	Creating Confidence.	40
26	Lifeless Limerence.	42
27	If A Man Can Do It, So Can I.	44
28	When Did Love Write A Rule Book?	46
29	My Heart Learned Not to Ache.	52
30	Anxious.	54
31	I Don't Want To Dilute Myself For You.	56
32	Dreamer. Drummer.	58
33	Pushy Placeholder.	61
34	Mixed Signals.	63
35	Disposable Yo-Yo.	65
36	Look Within First.	67
37	Heartbreak, Soul aches	69
38	Empty Within.	71
39	Today My World Is Black And White.	72
40	Marionette Doll.	74
41	Damning Gifts.	76
42	Empty Eyes.	77
43	Comforting Words, Painful Phrases.	79
44	Human Lie Detector.	80
45	Forever Strangers If You Don't Try.	82
46	Live A Life Romantic.	84
47	I Am Magical And Full Of Fire.	86
48	I Want To Fall.	88
49	I Want A Wild Life.	89
50	My Moon Gives Strength.	90
51	I Am A Gift.	91
52	Breakdown.	93
53	Glimpses Of Growth.	99
54	Is it me?	101

55	It Has To Be Me Right?	105
56	Borrowed Strength	107
57	Broken	112
58	What Is Love?	114

Acknowledgments

For Asher, who gave me purpose.
    For Spencer, who made me want to fight.
    For the men who said I was too much.
    That I wasn't enough.
    Critiqued all of my words.
    To the men who are teaching me to choose myself for once.
    For Simon, who inspired me.
    And told me not to dilute myself.
    My concentrated version is perfect.
    For Lindsay, who supported me.
    Who built me up.
    Who listened.
    You were a sister I didn't expect to find.
    For Tiffany, whose facial expressions validated me.
    Made me realize what I was saying and that I wanted to heal.
    For Hannah, who showed me renewed passion.
    For all the people who have felt less than enough.
    Or been told they are too much.
    You are enough.
    For anyone who has been kicked by love.
    Knocked down by life.
    For anyone who has been disappointed or letdown.
    You are more than enough.

Even if they can't handle your light.
Find someone who can.
Who brightens you.
Don't dilute yourself for anyone-
the concentrated version is what you deserve to show to the world.
Stay strong.
Stay beautiful.
Fly high little bird.
Show the world your strength.

1

Be Enough. You Aren't Too Much.

I had to learn to be enough because at some point,
   I knew I couldn't rely on anybody else.
   I love all and none simultaneously.
   I am learning to love me.
   I am learning to prioritize me.

2

The Stars Were My Friends.

When I had no one,
   I had the stars.
   I would whisper all my dreams.
   My fears, my wishes
   To any light that would twinkle my way.
   The stars would always listen
   To everything I thought would never be.
   I whispered love.
   I whispered loss.
   I would lay outstretched in the street
   Staring up at my friends who never laughed.
   They never judged.
   The stars would listen
   And glisten a silent message
   To keep going.
   Push harder and make things better.
   I discovered peace in the dark.
   The place that once filled me with fear

THE STARS WERE MY FRIENDS.

Now feels like where I belong.

3

Lack of Love, Mostly Malice.

Am I?
  Am I enough?
  Am I too much?
  Am I a saint?
  A sinner?
  Am I a healer?
  An artist?
  Who am I?
  I searched for love in all the wrong places
  Because I never got it from who I should
  I wasn't worthy of their love
  I wasn't who they said I should be
  My opinions didn't matter unless I conformed
  But no matter how pure I was, it didn't matter.
  The hoops I was given would always be pushed higher.
  It wasn't that I didn't reach the bar,
  It was that you didn't want me to.
  You don't love anyone

LACK OF LOVE, MOSTLY MALICE.

But you choose how you treat those around you
And you knew from day one I wasn't enough
Couldn't be. Wouldn't be.
You would hate anyone that offered a chance at me feeling genuine love.
Because you decided I didn't deserve it.
You could withhold what you didn't want me to feel
But you couldn't control others loving me
Unless you convinced me that no one was enough
Especially those who were more likely to make me strong.
You couldn't control others emotions
But you could try to poison who I let be in my circle
Your actions were insidious
And I cried as I tried to build healthy habits
Because I had never known anything without malice at its core.

4

Mockingbird. Fragile Bird.

We drove through the darkness
    Of the winding canyons in Utah
    Loud music blaring
    Chain Smoking Marlboro lights
    Until we came across a park
    We would sit in the swings
    And blow smoke into the night sky
    As we tried to blow away our cares.
    Instead the smoke filled our lungs
    And made it hard to breathe
    While providing fleeting comfort.
    We talked about everything and nothing.
    I watched her hands shake
    Difficult to light her next cigarette
    Despite being in her 20s.
    She showed me music
    And temporary acceptance.
    I broke it.

MOCKINGBIRD. FRAGILE BIRD.

I was unhealthy.
And I broke it.
But she introduced me
To many of my favorite things.
She felt like a bird.
Frail. Flighty. Fragile.

5

My Temple Has Stained Glass.

Your coveted temple walls
   Were white with frosted windows
   I chose to cover mine
   With graffiti art and stained glass
   My color initially made me hide
   But that art helped me choose life
   I wore my art like the proud peace
   I had spent years hiding from the world
   The tags I placed on my skin
   Became a map of each time I chose life

6

Pretended To Want Me.

It has always been clear that
    Sex is the only thing I am worth.
    You knowingly took from me.
    Knew I wasn't someone you wanted.
    But you strung me along.
    Giving enough effort
    To keep my interest piqued
    And legs spread.

7

Let The Games Begin.

I was on top of the world yet felt tiny inside.
  Invisible.
  But you reached your hand up and grabbed mine.
  I thought your imperfections made you more sincere.
  It felt like you were the first person to see me. To want me.
  I stood at the counter feigning confidence.
  Allowed to converse with men.
  My boss. His friends.
  Were you my friends?
  I wasn't included but kept close.
  But I felt your hand on the low of my back.
  I froze. Thinking you would stop.
  Maybe your actions were triggered by movement.
  If I stay still, he stays still.
  But it didn't work.
  I felt your hand slide down my pants.
  In my panties.
  I pulled away.

LET THE GAMES BEGIN.

    Even grabbed your arm.
    But you wouldn't budge.
    You took what you wanted.
    And so I froze again.
    Your fiance just left.
    We are surrounded by people and lights.
    And yet you take what you want.
    Does anyone see this?
    I look around and nothing changes.
    Their faces are blank. Talk continues.
    I squirm to leave but you hold me still.
    Taking what isn't yours.
    You finally let me leave.
    I walk off full of shame.
    But yet you follow.
    Asking. Pushing. Teasing.
    But you pile on shame
    That shouldn't be mine to bear.

His imperfect face turned back to me.
    The man who made me less invisible.
    He wanted me. Gave me attention.
    Asked me to stay behind.
    To help him close.
    A job he didn't need help with.
    When he got close,
    I could taste the Miller Lite and Marlboro
    He wasted time.
    I watchfully waited around.
    I needed to go but I couldn't bring myself to.
    Stayed by him. Flirted. Smiled.

He walked to the jukebox, chose many tunes.
I swooned when he let me pick too.
He went back to talking and mopping.
Aimlessly chatting.
A familiar tune started.
He dropped the mop and grabbed my hand.

If you fall, I will catch you
   He sang with her

I will be waiting.
   And danced with me.

My butterflies were unstoppable.
   He made a proposition
   That I wanted to refuse.
   But the music played.
   And we danced.
   I thought there could be romance.
   But he would want more that I hadn't given.
   So I said yes.
   Meekly.
   Barely any sound came out.
   He laid me down on the dirty green felt.
   Pulled off my pants
   And gave what I didn't want.
   I tried to turn my brain off.
   Be anywhere but there.
   All while trying to give him what he wants.
   I held my breath but all I heard was
   'What the fuck does it take to get you off?'

LET THE GAMES BEGIN.

His voice was full of frustration.
I don't know. I never have.
I said softly but he knew.
I tried to talk. Flirt.
He was cold when he stormed off.
We left and I ceased to exist.
He found someone new to keep him warm.
Her red mustang, nursing degree, beer belly.
His harsh behavior made me want to fix it more.
He would talk to me secretly.
Profess feelings he didn't show.
He invited me over to watch the Bills.
Wanted me undressed.
Promised his hands would not wander.
He never kept his word.
Just the tip. Just for a second, Just to see what it feels like.
I said no but was barely audible.
He was angry yet again.
I left and became more invisible.
A stain they forgot to clean up behind the bar.
He kept texting saying marriage and babies.
Always had a grand plan.
Made me listen to his self love
Before he disappeared finally forever.

8

No Means No, Even If Soft

I thought I was trying to heal for years
  But instead compensated better.
  I became stronger but I didn't face anything
  I didn't face my trauma.
  I didn't face my fears.
  I didn't set boundaries.
  I let people continue to use me.
  I made jokes to minimize my sadness
  So no one else could do it first.
  But now I heal.
  I talk. I confront. I cry.
  I found feelings again.
  I cry even when I'm not angry
  But for years anger was the only emotion I could muster.
  I deserve better.
  My future deserves better.
  So fuck you.
  Fuck you all.
  Fuck everyone who hurt me.

NO MEANS NO, EVEN IF SOFT

Broke me.
Made me hide.
I felt like I was in the wrong.
That maybe if my no had been louder
It would've meant more
And kept you from taking what you wanted.
No means no.
Even if it's soft.
Quiet.
Sad.
No means no.
But it never did to you.
To any of you.
I should've yelled and screamed.
But was taught your voice meant more.
You were the head and I was the neck.
I craved attention, but didn't want it like that.

9

Speak To Me.

Speak.
   Speak to me love,
   Speak to me fears.
   Speak what no one would.
   Tell me.
   Tell me how.
   How to be mine.
   Be yours.
   How to be someone worth pride.
   I was never the one anyone wanted.
   I was inconvenient.
   I love too hard.
   I feel too big.
   And all of that is just a facade
   As I hide my sadness behind a mask.

10

The Holes You Left Were Smaller.

You came into my life when I needed you most
   And deep down, I think you needed me too.
   You stayed until I loved myself,
   Before you slowly faded into the shadows.
   My questions were never fully answered.
   And you never let me in.
   My door was open and I welcomed you.
   But yours was only cracked.
   For the first time in a long time,
   I felt wanted, heard and adored
   Although it often felt like
   We were speaking different languages.
   I fell asleep most nights dreaming
   About the look of longing in your eyes.
   The look you said I wasn't supposed to see.
   I wanted to see the future
   But you drifted further out of sight.
   As you slipped away, I learned not to pull back.

A LIFE LESS BLACK AND WHITE

I had always lost the invisible game of tug'o'war
When I tried to keep people from leaving,
They chose to abandon.
You taught me to let them.
And I learned to let you go.
I loved myself enough to stand tall for once.
And what I will always remember is you gave me that.
You filled the large holes other people left behind
But in their wake you left smaller ones for me to repair.

11

I Fight.

The world works to tear me down
   And so, many days I fight
   To let my light shine.
   To be myself.
   To share all of me.
   But some days the world wins
   It beats me down
   Makes me feel like less.
   I'm never enough.
   I doubt love.
   I doubt in my ability to ever find it
   Will anyone ever understand me
   Want me to be myself
   And love me unconditionally
   Maybe he was right.
   Soulmates don't exist.
   The world isn't happy.
   It isn't what I make it out to be.

Maybe I am too optimistic.
Not realistic.
But then I find some small sign.
That the universe believes in me.
That it wants me to smile.
And so I fight.
I rise above.
I battle through another day.
I put on a smile.
Pull myself from the dark.
And act like someone I would be proud to know.
Because I am blessed.
Even if people try to tell me otherwise.

12

Stand Strong.

Stand Strong, little bird.
   They will try to ruffle your feathers.
   But aren't strong enough to pluck them.
   From the tough hide you grew.
   When the wind comes blowing.
   Begging to take you with it.
   Fly high, be free.

Fly high, little bird.
   Spread your wings.
   And soar above.
   Learn to leave
   These miserable depths
   Far below you.

Fly high, little bird.
   Be more than where you were planted.
   Find truth.
   Find love.

Find happiness.

Fly high, little bird.
   Be more than you can even dream.
   You were destined for greatness.
   But taught to expect leftovers.

Fly high, little bird.
   The world is vast.
   You deserve more.
   Earn more, be more.
   But do not accept less.

13

Sparrow's Song.

I watch the sparrow
   Sing to itself
   Even if no one hears its song
   The world bustles
   Around her nest
   And yet she sings.
   She doesn't soften
   Or budge
   She sings.
   Her song doesn't adjust
   To be something different.
   Even if the world pretends
   Not to hear
   She serenades herself
   And creates her own joy.

14

Hummingbird Wings.

Lean into life.
  Lean into love.
  Your fleeting chance.
  Flies fast like hummingbird wings.
  People will touch you
  And leave you.
  Without reason.
  They want a frightened bird.
  They want to be strong
  And leave you weak.
  Full of endless
  Hollow emptiness.
  But rise above
  And be more.

15

Lacking.

I looked up and realized life finally felt good.
   But it had been so hard, I wondered how that happened.
   I had tried earnestly to end it all.
   Because death was less painful than the future.
   Some days, I looked around
   To try and see if something was wrong.
   Were my surroundings correct?
   Or had I died and the Universe
   Wanted me to know what peace felt like.
   That was the only explanation some days.
   Why I would go from unhappy to content.
   But then it became more obvious.
   I was creating my own peace
   But the world was still full of pain.
   I refused to absorb what it threw my way.
   I had changed.
   I had grown.
   I became stronger externally

But remained fragile inside.

I knew she was missing.
   There was a hole in my home.
   I fought for her.
   And she came fiercely into the world.
   Her start was rocky.
   So I advocated harder.
   My decision had been so difficult before
   And I felt like this child was redemption.
   She was somehow a way
   To connect with my impossible past.
   I work so hard to prevent
   My kids from knowing lack
   That each day becomes filled
   With obligation and fatigue.
   Each decision I make will be wrong
   I want to give you what I never had
   But I struggle daily between knowing
   If you would rather have my time
   Or the comfort I never knew.

Time is valuable but so is security.
   I will fail no matter what I choose.
   So I struggle while you are young
   To set up your future.
   In your eyes, I see all my mistakes.
   And I know I fixed myself before you.
   But in your smile,
   I am aware of my improvement
   So I fight to be worth your joy.

LACKING.

There is never enough.
Never enough time.
My life is full of large aspirations
That I might never achieve.
I want to be the best for you.
I want to reach every target
That I was constantly told was too high.
I never worried about the distance
Until I was given the task to balance
My purpose and giving you the world.
The decision was impossible
But almost every other option was stolen.
I wanted you but didn't want myself yet
Then came redemption like you were mine again.

16

No One. Nothing.

Who am I?
    I am no one.
    Seeing nothing.
    Learning nothing.
    Being nothing.
    I used to drown in nothingness.
    But now I know,
    I am no one.
    I needed to find comfort alone.

17

Phoenix Rising.

What I think and what I know,
    You are a beautiful soul.
    You radiate sunshine but all I see are clouds.
    My hands are outstretched, eyes shut, face high.
    He promised love. Connection.
    Told me I rose above all obstacles.
    But pulled back. Shrank away.
    He was all talk. Never action.
    He wanted to put his burden on me.
    But gave me a slight glimmer of more.
    Made me think I might deserve better.
    He will never know
    He started my path of hope.

18

Palpable Air.

The air feels thick between us.
   Like the emotion is palpable.
   There is so much unclear
   But still so much has been said.
   Am I reading it wrong?
   Are these feelings one sided?
   How can we feel so close
   But be so far away?

19

Betrayed By Memory.

When I open my mouth, do words come out?
    My thoughts are constantly cut off by the rest of the world
    But when did you stop hearing me?
    When did my confidant decide
    That it wasn't worth listening to my thoughts?
    As I finally forgive myself of past mistakes
    I am starting to wipe the slate clean
    But instead of just forgetting the mistake,
    I find myself erasing most of my youth
    My memory lacks, despite my age.
    From so much misuse. Abuse. Fatigue.
    My memory lacks. It fails me often.
    As it attempts to protect me.
    My body chose to betray my mind
    That made me believe it was safe.
    My emotions had just turned numb
    After years of fighting and feeling
    And years of finding health.

Melancholy creeped up but I would've remained naive
Without my body's obvious treachery
My memories are fuzzy.
The details are faded.
Sometimes I catch bits and pieces
To let me know how bad things were.
I want to be strong but feminine.
I want to provide and be supported.
I am a walking contradiction.
And don't know how to accept the help
I have never been offered.
Let me love you.
But love me harder.

20

Screaming Silence.

I scream at the top of my lungs
   But all I produce is a squeak.
   I sob inwardly with forced stoicism.
   My body went numb. Emotions too.
   As soon as I lost the rest of my will.
   The illusion of freedom gave false hope
   And created painful gullibility.
   Everyone immediately awarded blind trust
   But none was earned.
   My soul became tired. Complacent. Docile.
   And I struggled to merit the love I was always told I would never deserve.
   I forgot all the memories that threatened my existence
   Although the underlying programming was securely laid
   The hidden message rang in my subconscious.
   You are nothing more than what I say.
   No one will ever be worth you
   Because you are worthless.

21

Give More.

Broken shoelace.
   Broken dreams.
   Dead ambitions.
   You drive me insane
   With your lack of care
   So all I can focus on is you.
   I deserve to focus on myself.
   I am more worthy
   Of the utter depth of my own love.
   I need to make you earn
   What I had to earn myself.
   But I gave you more than me.
   I should have ensured
   You wanted to be worthy
   Of the beauty I have to offer.
   I see the world differently.
   So why am I the only one chasing?
   Is it because you gave enough

GIVE MORE.

To keep me around.
So no one else could have me?

22

Shameless Remorse.

I am a fighter but I am no longer a child.
   I screamed silently into the abyss for years.
   I imagined my epitaphs in the rain.
   The ferns that once scared me no longer held power.
   They shriveled. Wilted. Died.
   Pain exists but only holds the power you give it.
   I once had a stream of sorrow
   That I hid from the world
   Thanking it made me strong.
   But it made me weak.
   Cracked my foundation over and over.
   You may never know my name.
   You may never know my meaning.
   I believe in everything.
   I believe in nothing.
   I am nothing yet I am everything.
   Everything is energy.
   I wait. Always waiting for something to happen

SHAMELESS REMORSE.

But nothing ever does.
I used to push my feelings down.
I pushed them away.
My feelings shrouded in shame.
They terrified me.
But I found bravery in facing them.

23

Fuck The Ocean.

Fuck the ocean.
   Behind its profound beauty is blind strength.
   Strength full of destruction.
   Strength full of rage.
   Accidental and intentional.
   Fuck the ocean.
   It separates land and love.
   Ignorance is bliss of what you're missing.
   Can you love what isn't there?
   Can you mourn what isn't known?
   And so I say with my words firm
   Watching him walk away.
   Fuck the ocean.

24

You Sparked Life Back Into Me.

Our time was short,
    You said it wasn't goodbye.
    That you would come back,
    But as I watched you walk away,
    I knew that wasn't true.
    Every time my camera clicks,
    I smile and remember you.
    I can't help but think of how you gave me confidence
    To share the parts of myself I hid away.
    I was enough. I was spectacular
    Like the bright sunsets I love to capture.
    I close my eyes to feel the sun warm my face.
    I wonder where you are.
    And whether you feel it too?

25

Creating Confidence.

I want to tell you everyday
   How much you drove me to try.
   To embrace my creativity.
   To show myself to the world.
   As everyone else told me to be less,
   You told me to be more.
   To be myself.
   I pretend to love less.
   Pretend to be less.
   But I am large.
   You told me to show myself.
   Offered support as I faltered.
   I found myself unbothered.
   Created a place of emotion
   That wasn't rooted in
   Letting others dictate how I feel.
   Or how much I show.
   But our distance is large.

CREATING CONFIDENCE.

The silence more vast.
So I hide myself less,
To show you what I can't say.

26

Lifeless Limerence.

Our infatuation is proper.
  I loved too big,
  For you.
  I loved too fast,
  For you.
  But toned it down.
  I feel too much
  But made my emotions smaller.
  I put a dampener on the love
  That I give to everyone.
  My love isn't bombing
  It is all encompassing
  But I put a bubble around you
  To shield from any discomfort.
  I had to find a version of myself
  That was acceptable to share.
  Will a time come where you are ready for all of me?
  I am a lot.

LIFELESS LIMERENCE.

I give.
I protect.
I heal.
I love.
I feel.
All while hiding parts of me
Behind tall walls.

27

If A Man Can Do It, So Can I.

I think I am finally falling in love with myself.
   But confidence feels so vain
   I decided to act like a man.
   Forgive myself.
   Absolve myself.
   Realize I can't do it all.
   Nor do I have to.
   I can focus on career
   And be the best mom.
   Providing in a way a man would
   Doesn't make me any less.
   Maybe my place isn't always in a kitchen,
   But leading meetings.
   Changing lives.
   Building something bigger.
   I don't have to be barefoot and pregnant
   To be a woman worth pride.
   They told me I wasn't enough

IF A MAN CAN DO IT, SO CAN I.

But too much simultaneously.
So I decided to say fuck it.
I am going to be me.
And that is worth loving,
Even if I'm the only one who does.

28

When Did Love Write A Rule Book?

When did love write a rule book?
   And every emotion become clearly defined
   The chance to feel.
   Express. Adore. Cherish.
   Feels policed by an invisible power.
   I love you.
   Because I love me.
   And internally I value you.
   You add merit to my life.
   To my soul. To my day.
   I want to be a better version of myself
   Just because I know you are around.
   But my speech isn't free.
   My emotions slip through at times
   And always wreak havoc.
   Cold, tall walls are safer than self expression.
   My self defense is my savior.
   Because when did love write rules?

WHEN DID LOVE WRITE A RULE BOOK?

Did love even have a say in its established decorum?
Are my flags red because I try to feel?
It always fails but yet I try.
Limerence. Infatuation.
They're words given to express untrue love.
But why can't I love without expectation?
Love should be pure.
It should be free.
If all you need is love,
Then why can't I give of myself
When my soul is on fire?
The love I received has always been taxed.
Or empty. Or unavailable.
Those closest to me did not give what my soul craved.
I have saved lives by loving freely.
Lifting those around me
Even if just mere acquaintances.
My healing hands and caring heart
Were always happy to give what no one gave me.
My broken heart could shelter yours
And keep it safe through the storm.
And so I love.
I love everyone even though
Most never make it past my walls
There are precious few that infiltrate
Where trust is extended
And safety attempted.
They are the only ones who can hurt me.
Because I allow them to see me without armor.
They see me from within the walls.
My guard is down.

And still I love.
But that love has rules
Rules I attempt to keep.
But I love hard. And deep.
And my love has hues.
It is a rainbow of depth
Instead of matching others monochrome emotions
My love shines. It permeates.
I give it freely whether deserved or not.
I offer what I did not receive
To try and connect.
And build. And grow.
I love myself.
I learned to. I had to.
I yearned. I struggled and fought.
But I chose me so that I could give love
Because what love I gave before
Chipped away and emptied my bucket.
Instead of sharing my self love,
I gave pieces of myself.
But now I love me.
I love my flaws.
I love my chaos.
But I don't know if someone else will.
Am I the problem?
Because I don't understand the decorum?
After a lifetime of having no love.
Or love with stipulations.
Love with manipulation.
Am I the problem for teaching myself?
Self taught what most people are shown.

WHEN DID LOVE WRITE A RULE BOOK?

To me love was pain.
Love was harsh.
Love was expected.
But now I found my rules.
I found my voice.
But my speech isn't free.
Words give me peace
But hurt me simultaneously
Just like everyone I have loved.
Eventually they all hurt you.
Their love is pain.
They leave you.
Betray your trust.
Or spit on your safety.
But still I love.
And love too hard.
I am too much for most.
I am too much for me sometimes.
I wanted to brand LOVE on my arm with pride
So I could wear it on my sleeve
But I looked within at my darkest time
And all I found was HATE.
Love hurt me so much
And yet when I was low,
I wanted it around with me always.
I wanted to show the world love.
But I looked down and hesitated,
Because what is love?
I didn't know.
I didn't know love
Because I didn't love me.

So how could anyone else?
I wanted to wear love as a badge of honor
But I couldn't think of anything true
So I cried and branded HATE
So everyone in my path could see
I knew I didn't deserve it's foe.
I earned HATE. Not LOVE.
I found my worth in time.
I chose me. And in doing so, I chose love
And made the choice to give what I never received
So no one else had to wear their self-loathing
Branded on their sleeve.
I covered my HATE with life.
Adding meaning to my stained glass.
It gave me pride in my skin again.
To hide the HATE I thought I deserved.
I give what I did not get.
Do I give too fast? Too open? Too much?
Probably.
I try to combat the poisoned breadcrumbs
I was fed my whole life
By giving more than enough to anyone I encounter.
I might not know you. But I love you.
Because love is light.
And I found my internal sunshine.
Whether romantic or platonic-
I feel with intention.
Openly to all.
Whether deserved or earned.
Given or taken.
I share my energy.

Whether understood or not.
I feel strongly.
I love hard.
To love. To be in love. To love yourself.
My love has hues.
Because I show my sunshine.
I share my light.
So no one has to sit alone in the dark.

29

My Heart Learned Not to Ache.

My heart learned not to ache.
  That aching doesn't help.
  Aching slows you down.
  My eyes are weak
  And betray my withheld emotion
  With endless tears, any chance they get.
  My heart doesn't ache anymore
  But my lungs will struggle to fill.
  My breath takes effort to catch.
  My heart doesn't ache anymore
  But my head pounds with incessant thoughts.
  A barrage of unkind words
  Or replaying melancholy moments.
  My heart doesn't ache anymore.
  My body betrays me and trembles.
  Usually overworked and undernourished.
  My heart doesn't ache anymore
  Because I have learned to compensate.

MY HEART LEARNED NOT TO ACHE.

Hiding my inner thoughts.
Hiding my feelings.
Mostly hiding me.

30

Anxious.

I closed my eyes and felt the familiar tug.
   My chest tightened.
   Breathing quickened.
   The memory was so fleeting
   I couldn't tell what it was.
   I dared to close my eyes again
   In an attempt to face whatever demon
   I felt pushing to come out.
   My demons had power when I hid from them
   But I was ready to face whatever was there.
   My hand pushed on my chest
   Reassuring my lungs to breathe.
   It isn't real, I thought.
   Whatever it is can't hurt you anymore.
   You're safe. You're grown.
   Close your eyes and see
   Whatever is trying to haunt you.
   It only has the power you give it now.

ANXIOUS.

I slowed my breaths
And dared myself to close my eyes.
I couldn't heal if I didn't know
What hidden memory was tormenting me.
The ground started to fall away from beneath my feet.
My eyes closed, hand pressed firm.
It helped to soothe my troubled mind.
I rose higher and higher in the air.
All while searching again
For the beast that threatened my well being.
But I felt his hand grasp mine
And rub circles on my thumb.
But he never knew what I saw.
What I felt. What I was facing.
Yet his grip never loosened.
Never stopped silently letting me know
That he was there. That I was safe.
When I found the hidden memory,
I faced it head on.
And found no pain in it anymore.
I found calm before I opened my eyes.
His thumb still calmly drawing circles on my skin.
But when vision cleared, eyes opened
I saw a rainbow of colors in the sunrise.
Felt his safe grip on my hand
And knew I was right to call my power
To appreciate the gift from the universe
That I found in another magnificent morning.

31

I Don't Want To Dilute Myself For You.

I smiled warmly as he talked
   Fully aware that I had watered myself down.
   My walls were up halfway
   To preemptively protect my heart.
   I no longer felt seen.
   And so I diluted myself.
   A watered down version
   That was more palatable for most.
   Very few were willing to drink from my fire hose.
   To see me as I am.
   Those that did, found love.
   Acceptance. Connection.
   But there was a world not ready for me.
   And although I never understood why,
   I found a way to make myself less.
   I maintained myself internally
   And showed that light to a select few
   After clearly showing they didn't need shade.

I DON'T WANT TO DILUTE MYSELF FOR YOU.

They adored the version most true to me.
I was still finding who I was,
But that journey was turbulent.
It was filled with emotions
Most people didn't want this version.
And yet it was the most authentic.
So what happens when I find who I truly am?
Who can handle me concentrated?
If diluted was already hard to grasp
Do I shut out the rest of the world?
Give up on love?
Partnership?
I already questioned soul mates
After having candidates respond
That my glass was too full.
People were too evil.
The world was too harsh.
And true love didn't exist.
Then what was I clinging to?
What hope was left?
There had to be something larger.
Something to make me work
To grow. To find truth.
But I knew when to dilute
In an attempt to stop chasing off
Those who didn't know more existed.
Unknowingly trying to decipher
If anyone would ever be ready
To put me on an earned pedestal
And love my plentiful flaws.

32

Dreamer. Drummer.

Some days I pine for imagined emotions.
   I close my eyes after waking.
   Wishing myself back into my dream.
   Reality is colder than my imagination
   And I have been chasing the warmth
   I felt from fictitious people
   While dreaming of what I long to find.
   I sat next to him on the ground while he worked
   Because he couldn't stand to be away.
   I could see him glance down
   Smile and rub his thumb across my cheek.
   But my eyes opened too soon.
   I squeezed them closed to try and leap back
   Into a dream I knew I could never recreate.
   The warmth was real.
   The loss felt catastrophic.
   There was an instant hole in my chest
   When I knew my brain wouldn't give me another second of

that love.
   He was gone forever.
   Even though the person was fiction,
   The moment was fleeting,
   And it was all a dream–
   There were days, weeks, months, even years
   That I longed for someone to care.
   To caress my cheek and adore me.
   My mind created what I needed.
   To fill the holes that caused my heart to leak
   But my brain didn't realize the tear it made
   In my delicate fortress.
   You don't crave what you don't know,
   As hard as you crave what is lost.
   The lost love was never more than a dream.
   But I wanted him to appear.
   Wanted someone to cherish my soul.
   To love my contradictions.
   I was fragile yet resilient.
   I was loving yet guarded.
   I protected others at all costs.
   I needed a shiny knight for myself
   But would never be vulnerable enough
   To admit I needed help.
   To admit I wanted more.
   To admit I felt like I deserved what others had
   But wouldn't advocate to find.
   And so I was content.
   Hollow yet happy enough
   With what I was handed.
   With what I found.

I built a scrapyard
With the bits and pieces I was given.
No one offered themselves whole.
Instead they gave me what they had leftover.
Their extras. Their spare parts, not in use.
But the effort was absent.
And they only gave what didn't take away from them.
Because everyone else is their own first priority.
But I pour my cup out into others who need.
I give to those I love even if met with hurt in the future.
My cup needs to be refilled often and I occasionally have a dry base.
But I give.
I give to everyone.
As soon as we meet,
I can feel their soul to know where they lack.
And so I give them what they need.
Even if I give my last because I know they need it
And I can always survive.
I know I fight but others aren't as strong.
Resilience is learned through trauma
And not everyone had to fight to rise.
So I give knowing I can make more.
And give too much again to the next person in need.

33

Pushy Placeholder.

There is service in your acts
    But lack of communication.
    My words are often judged.
    Questioned.
    Lessened.
    My meaning called to be less than intended.
    Sometimes seen as more than I meant.
    But it is always something I need to defend.
    You speak openly of your past
    But judge mine.
    Contradiction is standard.
    What I say is often different than what you hear.
    When I say daisy, you hear daffodil.
    Because that is what you expect me to be.
    Your notions seem preconceived.
    Then why stay?
    Because you tell me constantly
    That you're the one who leaves.

You break things at the first sign of incompatibility.
So why stay?
I don't know that I will ever fit into your created glass bubble.
You tell me about your exes and what made them imperfect.
All I feel is the measuring tape as you size me up next to them.
This one was too crazy.
This one was too sane.
This one wanted money.
This one's to blame.
But how do I fit in?
With my self proclaimed, loved imperfections.
Will you ever see the value I bring?
Or continue to try and make me what you want.
You confidently say some crazy is okay.
Some sane too.
But you want sex and money.
A woman who can do it all.
Someone worthy of you.
I need to be worthy of me too.
This feels one sided.
There was a time it would have been enough.
But not now. Not here.
Not with this version of me.
I fought to find myself.
To give myself more.
And I have to stop accepting less.

34

Mixed Signals.

Today you showed me a side that no one gets to see.
   You confided.
   Showed me vulnerability.
   And told me things you never admit.
   You're stoic.
   Strong.
   Dependable.
   But today you admitted that there are times you're not.
   You've wanted to quit.
   Step down and take less responsibility.
   But will never tell others so that they can use your strength.
   You showed me casual.
   Friendly.
   Fun.
   We didn't have to put on a show.
   But instead enjoyed being with each other.
   No impressing.
   No flourishes.

But just imagining what every day could be.
Your touch warms my skin and my heart
And makes me wonder what could be.
But deep down, I always ponder
Will I ever fit into your life's puzzle?
Our pieces click together simply
Despite differences, misunderstandings and miscommunications
But will I ever be someone you show to the world?
Will you find a platform to put me on?
Or will you continue to hide me away?
Wondering if I am worthy of you.
Worthy of meeting your family.
Worthy of meeting your friends.
Worthy of being on your arm.
And so I sit and ponder if nights like this will be sustained.
Or if this will be all we ever are.
You tell me of your people who matter but they don't know I exist.
And I have to wonder if they ever will or if I will always be your secret.
Our opinions are different.
Our timelines don't match.
Even our ideas are not the same.
I want to come out of the shadows.
But instead sit patiently in the wings to see what I get to be.

35

Disposable Yo-Yo.

I know I am your secret
   And I am little but not dirty.
   You swipe away any messages
   Out of respect? Out of secrecy?
   You pull me close so you can push me away.
   I feel like a yo-yo in your hands.
   If I express something wrong,
   I am thrown away.
   Try again and maybe I will pull you back.
   But with each throw, I stay farther away.
   The distance grows but it should lessen.
   We are together but am I enough?
   We were more before but now grow to be less daily.
   We have no consistency but you're content
   As I bend to fill the gaps I am permitted,
   I have to mold myself to fit where you allow.
   But how dare I try to define.
   I'm not upset anymore.
   I mask my emotions unsure if they're allowed.

My leg shakes but I stay composed and continue the conversation
  Because I am not supposed to be difficult.
  Affable is preferred.
  I need to be casual.
  Calm.
  You hold my bag.
  Open the door.
  You are a gentleman but how much is mine?
  I feel we should have more.
  I need emotion.
  Passion.
  I feel like a burden at times.
  You keep me close but at a distance.
  I am allowed to be where you feel comfortable.
  And so with each throw, I come back less and less.
  Is it my walls keeping me from rebounding to you?
  Or is it your lack of care?
  You open up.
  Tell me I am your confidant.
  Although admitting there was intent
  Behind taking away my precious communication.
  You agree we had more.
  We were more.
  But you pulled back.
  Because I love so much,
  You push but don't pull me back as hard.
  You let me stay farther away each time.
  With each throw I know, I am your yo-yo.
  A play thing at your discretion.

36

Look Within First.

I am enough for me.
   Not for you.
   You give breadcrumbs
   When I ask for loaves.
   I might be enough for me.
   But you're not enough for me.
   You willingly take away from me
   You say I am imperfect.
   Find a mirror, sweet friend.
   Commitment isn't scary,
   If you look at yourself first.
   I am enough.
   Not too much.
   Goldilocks would like me.
   But you never will.
   You need to practice what you preach.
   What you tell me I am not.
   Always telling on yourself

When telling me to be more.
Do you hate my fire?
My fight?
My drive?
Do you loathe my confidence?
The fact that I am learning where to thrive.
And everyone else bends backwards to want you.
But I know you don't give enough.
You break it, you buy it.
You didn't buy me,
But you broke me.
You didn't want me.
You showed me.
You kept me here.
In secret.
Your pretty secret.
But I deserve more.
Even if I give it to myself.

37

Heartbreak, Soul aches

This is the most perfect night and yet my soul aches.
    My heart unsure of what it needs to be whole.
    To be happy.
    To feel seen.
    Are my needs met?
    Am I asking too much?
    Does he want to shower me with adoration?
    Or is this just a different flavor
    Of each man who has been here before?
    A richer flavor but still not full bodied.

Why is my soul aching?
    It feels earnest yet empty.
    Incomplete.
    But doesn't know where it is lacking.
    It feels safe to give less and say others are too much.
    But if you never give of yourself, you'll never know what you're missing.

You can't be whole without being vulnerable.
You want to be safe.
You want to be careful.
But love is messy.
Love is hard.
It's painful.
And it fucking hurts.
So you can't find love without losing a little bit of yourself.
You should love yourself first,
But not always more.
Find someone to give of yourself.
Find someone worth sacrifice.
But know that you are content alone.
So that when you choose to give,
Everything you are to someone,
You know it's actually real.

38

Empty Within.

My head isn't sad
   My heart isn't broken
   So how do I describe this feeling?
   I am lonely yet surrounded.
   I am not happy.
   I am not sad.
   I know what I am not,
   But I do not know what I am.
   My soul feels empty.
   My bucket dry.
   I feel void of anything.
   I feel nothing.
   A blank slate of uncertainty.

39

Today My World Is Black And White.

Today my world is black and white.
   The threat of color stings.
   I see so many hues naturally.
   But today everything is shades of grey.
   Monochrome.
   Bleak.
   Every image seems better when it's drained of every shade.
   Today my world is black and white.
   I walk alone.
   Explore the city while you sleep.
   This was supposed to be for us.
   But you minimize saying it was for you.
   Travel is nothing.
   Nothing to you.
   To me it is life.
   It is everything.
   And so my color shuts off.
   And my world is black and white.

TODAY MY WORLD IS BLACK AND WHITE.

I find adventure with myself.
Prefer my company alone
Since you start to minimize me.
Today your company makes me less.
Makes the gesture nothing.
But I am everything.
And even though this is nothing to you.
It gives me goals.
To travel alone.
See the play alone.
To meet my goals alone.
Find new places.
New experiences.
Alone.
Because I deserve more.
I deserve the effort I give the world.
You should fight to match me.
Exceed me.
But you don't.
So this isn't it.
I like you.
I love you.
Those words scare you
So I hide them.
I hide myself.
For a moment,
I act like you aren't there.
And my heart is more full.

40

Marionette Doll.

I opened my book and dared to have confidence.
   Unapologetically pulled out a pen
   To write in the margins of my life.
   You said all the right things.
   Told me you wanted to be a safe space,
   All while pulling away.
   Your messages were mixed.
   You want a life partner.
   You acted like you wanted to be with me.
   But it became evident you didn't.
   Your effort was lackluster.
   I accepted you for who you were.
   But you never offered me the same.
   You let me stand on the promise of safety,
   But then pulled the rug out from under me,
   As soon as you felt unsure.
   You wrapped a string around my arms,
   And kept me dancing like a marionette.

MARIONETTE DOLL.

I shouldn't have felt so free to cut those ties.
To break things with someone I liked.
But you didn't want me authentically.
For once, I chose me.
I knew I deserved more.
I don't know everything I want,
But I know the effort I deserve.
And you took it away while pretending to be all in.

41

Damning Gifts.

He unknowingly gave me the most damning gifts of all.
 Confidence.
 Hope.
 Happiness.
 Contentment alone.
 Since he fought to avoid me,
 I knew I would be happier without him.
 He gave me something I struggled to give myself.
 And I finally saw that I deserved more than he would ever offer.

42

Empty Eyes.

Your eyes lack the look I have been chasing,
    Since the wrong person showed me it existed.
    It was accidental.
    Fleeting.
    Barely there.
    If I blinked, I would have missed it.
    For the first time I saw longing.
    I saw lust.
    I saw love in another human's eyes.
    The gaze was directed at me.
    And finally I understood.
    But your eyes are empty.
    There is no gaze.
    You don't seem to penetrate my soul with a single glance.
    And so I know, it isn't you.
    It can't be him either
    But I know it isn't you.
    And so I search for another human

Capable of reproducing the fleeting look of pure love.

43

Comforting Words, Painful Phrases.

I walked in and was met with familiarity.
   The smell was comforting,
     As I smiled at all of the old friends staring at me.
   Words hurt from those around me,
   But these old friends never wanted blood.
   They were steadfast.
   A constant presence in my life.
   There was never a moment they abandoned me.
   If I needed release, I could grab my friend
   And bury myself in their world for a bit.
   I wanted to know their woes,
   As a comforting way to avoid mine.
   I would always smile as I read their thoughts.
   I was reassured I would always know the ending to their story,
   Since mine was still being written.

44

Human Lie Detector.

I hear it all.
   I hear what is not said.
   I hear the wind.
   I hear your thoughts.
   I hear each shift in your mood.
   I had to learn to know
   What everyone was thinking.
   I had to know what wasn't said.
   There was always anger in the silence.
   There was so much left unanswered.
   I was made to decipher
   What I didn't understand.
   Why was everyone so silent?
   Silence.
   Painful Silence.
   Full of words not said.
   Hidden messages always lurking.
   Answers full of hesitation.

HUMAN LIE DETECTOR.

As you pick your words
To make yourself the hero.
Because you are never wrong.
But love robs you.
It empties you.
Takes all you have,
Before telling you it wasn't enough
It is never enough.
But always too much.

45

Forever Strangers If You Don't Try.

You're right.
   We don't know each other.
   We are strangers.
   Slowly learning.
   But you're right.
   Fuck my ideals.
   My dreams.
   Clearly.
   We don't know each other.
   I don't want your praise.
   I did but now I detest it.
   I needed validation.
   I wanted affection.
   But you make me loathe compliments.
   They are nothing.
   They are nothing alone.
   And you give nothing.
   Making me feel less than worthy

FOREVER STRANGERS IF YOU DON'T TRY.

Since I asked you to meet my needs.

46

Live A Life Romantic.

I want to find a world where I soak up the sun and creativity.
   Chase my dreams. Euphoric.
   Chase creativity I never imagined.
   There is a life, romantic.
   That would never be mine.
   It would never be obtained.
   But today I had a glimpse.
   Of a future life romantic.

I close my eyes and imagine being across the world.
   Peaceful.
   Alone.
   Full of whimsy.
   But open my eyes.
   Transported back to a job
   I didn't want anyway.
   I don't want to heal everyone anymore.
   When did I become the solution

LIVE A LIFE ROMANTIC.

But the fault in their problems?

Give me peace to create art.
   And fuck the world.
   I don't want to fix them anymore.
   They hate my loving too big.
   They say I am too much.
   As a way to excuse their constant lack.

My mind wanders endlessly
   Full of ideas and hope.
   But it is not allowed to capture.
   My thoughts are so fleeting.
   They hasten away before
   My pen can hit the paper.

47

I Am Magical And Full Of Fire.

Do you write what you know?
   Or what you don't?
   Do you share your dreams?
   In hopes they become reality?
   You chase sanity,
   Yet call me insane.
   I might be mad,
   But there is life in crazy.
   My fire burns daily.
   Most reach to light theirs from it.
   I feel it.
   I am lit from within.
   I am strength.
   Sad strength.
   But strength nonetheless.
   I grow stronger daily.
   My sadness powers me.
   I learned to fight from my trauma.

I could have given up a thousand times
But I chose to rise higher each time.
And so my fire burns.
Lit within from my aspirations.
Even if never achieved,
I know I will never hide from a challenge.
I will always face it head on.
What do I have to lose?
I will always fail if I never try.
But if I try, I can always succeed.
Even if success is learning a lesson
From my missed opportunity.
I learned to get up.
I learned to rise up.
I learned to fight another day.

48

I Want To Fall.

I watch a plane free fall from my window.
   With intentional reckless abandonment.
   I watch and I wish I could leap.
   I want to feel the wind soar past me.
   Let me fly.
   The clouds can be my pillow
   And I fly to them as they billow below me.

49

I Want A Wild Life.

I am proper yet pine for a wild life.
   Exploration.
   Freedom.
   Wings with almost no roots.
   I want to write in a new cafe each day.
   I want to see the world.
   I want to shirk my responsibilities
   And be like those who chase their dreams.
   It doesn't have to be pretty to love the way it feels.

50

My Moon Gives Strength.

I step outside and feel the wet air.
  I take a deep breath and feel condensation fill my lungs.
  I step out into the street, my arms outstretched
  Ready to scream if it wouldn't frighten the neighbors.
  I find strength in nature.
  The moon would light the way just enough,
  If I choose to open my eyes.
  I choose to walk in darkness at midnight.
  I walk, eyes closed.
  Music so loud in my ears I might go deaf.
  But would smile as each sound faded away,
  Because it filled my soul with strength.
  I could find joy in the sound of silence,
  Knowing I chose it for myself.

51

I Am A Gift.

I finally realized
   To know me is a privilege
   Not a right.
   To know my thoughts,
   To know my plans,
   To know my updates,
   Is a privilege.
   You don't get to insult me anymore.
   You don't get to placate me
   And pretend it isn't degrading.
   I am not a child.
   I am a full grown woman,
   Who has evolved more than you ever will.
   To know me is a gift,
   And you don't get it anymore.
   It is freeing to not have to pretend to be perfect anymore.
   I am messy.
   I am imperfect.

I am chaotic.
But I am making my own choices for once.
And you don't get to criticize me for it.

52

Breakdown.

I made it in the safety of my car before my eyes betrayed me.
    The tears blurred my vision as soon as the door closed.
    I had been holding my breath so that I could cry in peace.
    I made it home before I felt a second wave.
    I could feel the tightness in my chest and I knew it was coming.
    And the realization hit that he wasn't there to rub circles on my hand anymore.
    That it was my choice.
    Was it the right choice?
    I don't even know anymore.
    I know I can't tell him that.
    He would say I love too hard.
    Too fast.
    It would minimize my emotions.
    My longing. Missing him.
    It would prove his point.
    It was easy to be lonely even together since he pulled away.
    But I still knew deep down he was there.

He was there in silence but now he was actually gone.
He was no longer mine.
He wasn't mine for long and if I told him this,
I would be too attached.
Too codependent.
He would whittle down the time we spent together.
Like counting down to blastoff.
He always changed time to fit his point.
Probably unintentionally.
I know what we had was new.
But I was all in.

Is it codependent to want someone?
  A person to tell your things?
  The people who claim to be there aren't.
  Not really.
  One is absent when you need her.
  Too busy with her own concerns.
  But that isn't wrong.
  She tries to convince you to have emotions.
  You have a village.
  But then she shrinks away when you're in need.
  One accidentally insults your progress.
  One diminishes your words.
  With a pat on the head and attaboy.
  Is it wrong to want a person?
  A confidant.
  He said he wanted to be a safe space.
  But then he pulled away.

And so I sit and sob

BREAKDOWN.

   Realizing I am alone.
   I have my perfect kids.
   But I am alone.
   I don't have a person to rely on.
   If I called at midnight,
   No one would answer
   Especially if they don't even answer a text.

I sit in the shower and let the water run on my chest.
   Because I felt my air constricting
   And knew he wasn't there.
   No one was.
   But the hot pressure might help.
   I felt the water run cold.
   Before I dared to stand up but tears hit me again.
   So I stood with my head in the water,
   Trying to gain composure
   And welcomed back the robot.
   My walls that protected me for so long.
   If I don't feel the need to express myself,
   Then maybe I won't miss them.
   I don't need people if I don't have emotions to process.
   I realized that's why it doesn't feel like Christmas
   Normally it was my favorite time of year.
   Full of togetherness.
   Laughing. Longing. Loving.
   In theory.
   I always felt a little lonely this season
   A deep feeling of homesick despite being home.
   But the loneliness was closing in.
   Creeping closer.

It didn't bother me much before.
But that was when my walls stood tall.
Stood high. My fortress.
And I knew it was my fault I tore them down.
My fault.
I wanted to heal.
I wanted to be better.
Stronger.
And in the meantime, I realized I was totally alone.
The thought had been creeping in.
But here it was full force.
Nowhere to hide any longer.

The universe turned cruel.
   It reminded me more of him
   As I stared at the mirror and dried off.
   His song played.
   I found my note cards of questions
   From when he wanted to interview
   For the head of my fan club.
   I read our conversations with fresh eyes.
   And the tone had changed so much.
   Sex ruins everything.
   I know my broken self ruined it too.
   Not understanding healthy.
   Not knowing normal.
   I thought he would give me some grace.
   Because he wanted to be safe for me.
   But I opened up.
   Made mistakes.
   And he pulled away.

BREAKDOWN.

I changed myself.
Censored myself.
Kept some feelings at bay.
But he pulled back more.
I couldn't be any less without ceasing to exist.
How did we go from there to here?
I know we lost what it was
But where exactly did it go wrong?
He blamed me.
Quoted fear that we would move further
And not match each other.
But I felt like my heart was torn.
I was sad.
But more than that,
I felt alone.
The deep loss
That comes with the realization
That you can't have what wasn't yours.
I have been alone
But cared less because I was numb to it.
Every step has mattered
But today it hit me.
I am alone.
How do most people handle it?
Is it because you aren't addressing
A lifetime of emotions and learning
All at the same time?
I don't know healthy communication.
I don't fully understand emotions.
I don't understand partnership.
But I can't keep having the lessons

Thrown in my face as I am learning.
Let me learn.
Teach me.
Show me.
But please stop reminding me
Of every way I stumble as I learn to walk.
I want to be healthy.
I want to be good.
For me.
For you.
But I can't do that without help.
And so I sit in the realization.
That I am totally alone.
Stuck with my own
Dangerous thoughts and feelings.
Utterly Alone.

53

Glimpses Of Growth.

I feel like my brain is throwing puzzle pieces at me
   To help me better understand myself.
   Giving me flashes of what can be
   With flashes of what was.
   And so I sit.
   I shimmer.
   I glisten.
   Basking in my growth.
   On paper he was perfect
   But he wasn't perfect for me.
   He tried to say his growth
   Was what I should be.
   My path is too imperfect.
   My timing is too quick.
   I codepend. I need.
   But I found my lessons more quickly with him.
   I saw the flags that might be different shades for others.
   But to me, they billow crimson in the wind.

He made me feel so small.
But that's where he wanted me.
Under him.
I don't need to reflect.
Or have you show me what lessons I learned.
Because I found them on my own.
For the very first time, I didn't need opinions.
I knew I needed more.
I knew he wouldn't give it.
I had already changed so much
That if I made myself any less
He wouldn't see me.
Or hear me.
At all.
And I would fade off as if I never existed.
So I stood strong.
Said no thank you.
And held my decision even with all the reminders.
He might be Mr. Right for someone.
But he isn't mine.
Maybe if we learned to communicate.
But he didn't want all of me.
He needed sunglasses.
A visor. Shades.
I was too much.
Too bright.
He was drawn to my energy
But got burned the closer he came.

54

Is it me?

Why does 'no' never matter?
    Were you trying to prove your affection?
    Or were you meeting your own needs.
    You wanted to show me pleasure.
    Get me off.
    But you didn't know me yet.
    I said slow down
    But you still pulled off my pants.
    I said stop
    But you still thrust in.
    I said no
    But you acted like you didn't hear me.
    I said ow.
    I said that hurts.
    But you didn't slow down.
    I tried to use my words
    Despite the pattern being familiar
    But you didn't hear me.

I kept reaching.
I tried to pull your hand away.
But you pushed it in harder.
I tried to get you to stop.
But you wouldn't.
I could hear his voice
In the back of my head saying
What the fuck does it take to get you off?
You wouldn't stop.
Even when I tried to pull you away
I froze. Confused. Panicked.
What is happening?
I say it hurts but you keep going
Usually I am numb.
But this is pain.
You keep wanting me to finish.
And saying no didn't make you stop.
Pulling you away didn't help.
So I freeze.
Why does this keep happening?
Am I imagining things?
Making it worse than it is?
But I said no.
I used my words.
I used my hands.
But maybe too soft.
My no sounded stronger.
But it didn't matter.
You say you want another chance.
You will be offended if my body says no again.
You want me to come back willingly

IS IT ME?

Or you will lock me away in your dungeon.

You text me later
   Ask if you will see me.
   I give the benefit of the doubt
   That you obviously don't deserve.
   Try to tell you the hurt you caused.
   But your response says it all.
   You tell me I am not worth as much
   As your t-shirt I wore home.
   I planned to wash it. Return it.
   But yet you say-
   Give me a break
   You shouldn't have stolen my clothes.
   Look up theft.
   You're the only one who did anything wrong.
   Now I see why your husband
   Couldn't tolerate you.
   I can't believe I was dumb enough
   To let you leave with that shirt.
   You are not a good person.

I am wrong for being assaulted.
   I am wrong for speaking my concerns.
   Trying to talk it out.
   Thinking you had a soul.
   But every move was calculated.
   So says everyone.
   Yet this heartlessness is what I know.
   And you say I am a liar.
   You say I am the problem.

A LIFE LESS BLACK AND WHITE

You say a lot to cover your tracks
Because I am worth less than your shirt.

Even with these words
   Really despite your actions
   I am somehow fine.
   Cannot bring myself to report it.
   Just knowing how things work
   Or your legal connections.
   Has me worried to tell authorities.
   And I know I should say something
   Never wanting this to happen to anyone but
   Never wanting to see you again.
   So I wrestle with the choice
   And knowing the right answer
   Makes my indecision even harder.

55

It Has To Be Me Right?

I wasn't chasing
   I was searching
   Looking for someone
   Who created a feeling.
   Something I hadn't known
   Safety was love.
   But that isn't what I knew.
   Pain was what felt familiar.
   Did safety exist?
   I kept trying to heal
   But fell back in.
   Found an old pattern.
   Someone who seemed to want more.
   More than sex. More than my body.
   But he didn't. Saying no meant nothing.
   He took what he wanted.
   I have to be the problem
   But my body was covered.

No suggestion or touch.
But he kissed and took.
And all I could see was the first time.
I never felt like a victim
But knew it wasn't right.
Knew my body went numb.
Emotions gone.
But he was just like the first time.
Except worse.
My voice was louder.
More sure.
I said no.
I said slow.
I said stop.
I said ouch.
I pulled.
I pushed.
But he didn't stop.
He didn't ask.
He took what wasn't his.
How do I find safety?
When this is what finds me.

56

Borrowed Strength

I dream as I drive
   Dream of days past.
   Dream of days present.
   Dream of days future.
   I gaze ahead
   And the sky appears to burn
   With the trees topped in crimson
   Fading north into green, blue and black.
   My mind always wanders.
   Never able to be quiet.
   Constantly thinking.
   But my thoughts are peaceful as I drive.
   Peaceful because you are my destination.
   There's so much out of my control.
   My helpless being tries to ponder every outcome.
   Every idea feels like a solution,
     to the concern that plagues me.
   But I drive to him.
   Our future has never felt certain

But we know today, here and now
That we are each other's.
I am yours.
You are mine.
I see love behind your eyes.
But will we have a future?
You saw my uncertainty from the first moment.
And told me you were there.
That you would be there.
And that you hoped I would follow.
But did you mean it?
Were you sincere?
No one else had been.
But are you?

Your face beams when you catch my eye.
    I am afraid to look in case the moment passes.
    I stare ahead but I see you smile and watch.
    From the corner of my eye, I can feel your joy.
    Your acts of service are filled with love.
    You give disclaimers,
    Not to eat if I don't like it.
    And every time it makes me think
    Of my Southern Grandmother.
    Always serving with love.
    Convinced it was never enough.
    You laugh every time I look your way,
    Because I can feel your gaze.
    Warming my skin.
    Is that love?
    Do you feel it?

BORROWED STRENGTH

My heart is scared.
Uncertain.
Healing.
You help me see my flaws,
Just so I can heal.
Because I told you I wanted it.
Your perspective was a puzzle piece
That I had lost the ability to see.
You helped me know.
I wasn't wrong.
I wasn't lying.
They hurt me because I was soft.
I fought to please everyone.
Putting my own needs last.
Everyone with a beating heart,
Came before what I needed.
But not you.
You want me happy.
Healthy and strong.
I pretended to be fierce
But with you holding me up,
I might not need to feign strength.
You lent me yours.
You made me want to be whole.
For me.
For you.
For them.
How can I know if this might be forever?
Yet I am so terrified waiting for the inevitable.
Everything good comes to an end.
For me, everything bad ends,

Before I know it's bad.
Everyone leaves.

I see more and more, that I am truly alone.
    I feel it less with you but you encourage me.
    You help me find my strength so I can stand strong.
    Falter less.
    Be my own solidity.
    I wanted to be mighty.
    I wanted to be everything.
    Everyone relies on me constantly.
    A masquerade of attributes I want to embody.
    I wanted to fake it until I could make it.
    I didn't know how much I lacked until you helped me see.
    I couldn't sleep and I finally opened up.
    There was so much I couldn't say.
    The words were hiding but as I drove, I found them.
    I was sleepless.
    I wanted you to know the ways I found to help myself.
    So I thought.
    I decided.
    I told you my truth.
    You are wrong in all the right ways.
    You say you are hard, rough, strong.
    But for me you are soft.
    Gentle.
    Kind.
    Protective.
    You are everything I was scared to want.
    You are what I was scared to need.
    Yet the feeling I get with you is real.

BORROWED STRENGTH

Knowing that makes me more worried,
As we wait and see if we get a chance of a future.

57

Broken

You broke me.
 You broke me.
 And it hurt worse because I thought you were different.
 I thought my choice was better.
 Now I open my mouth and the words I want to say won't come out.
 I want to say them with conviction.
 I want to say them with intention.
 I know they are there.
 It hurts to hold them in.
 I can feel them.
 But all I can imagine is you pulling away.
 And the image of possible rejection,
 Hurts worse than keeping my truth locked away.
 I have new fears that everyone will run.
 Everyone left before and now I cannot utter the words.
 The timing was off but I was healing.
 Accidents happen.
 Vulnerability was always scary but now it feels impossible.

BROKEN

All I hear is your voice.
Judging my timing.
Questioning my feelings.
Pulling away.
I told you it shouldn't be this hard.
Not this early.
And you agreed.
But now I lost my strength to speak.
I lost my strength to feel openly.
The words used to flow out of my lips
Like a brook that babbles.
My feelings are there but are impossible to share.
My walls are up protecting the part of my heart,
I didn't know you broke.

58

What Is Love?

Love is reciprocation
    Being together solves most of it
    If that is what your soul craves.
    But mine needs words.

I come from nothingness
    And will leave the same.
    Who am I?
    I am no one.
    Never in love.
    Wanting.
    Waiting.
    But I have glimpses of hope.
    I refuse to settle.
    I will not accept less than deserved affection.

I have no desire to stop.
    I have no desire to be less.

WHAT IS LOVE?

I have no desire to settle.
So I will continue to fight.
I will rise.
I will grow.

You judge my timeline and say it is too fast.
    I rush because I know what I want.
    So why slow my progress to fit your comfort level?
    I want to grow.
    I want to rise.
    I want to be more.

I started from nothingness
    But I will end full of joy.
    I am no one.
    But that is enough for me.
    My words mean nothing,
    And everything simultaneously.
    I want to share them.
    You might know my thoughts.
    You might know my feelings.
    You might know my doubts.
    You might know my fears.
    You might even share some of them.
    And so I give my words to the world.
    They are small.
    But I thought I was small.
    I was wrong.
    I am finding my voice.
    Finding my healing.
    I am not small.

I am large.
I am no one.
I am me.
And finally...
I love me.

Made in the USA
Columbia, SC
03 February 2025